GRANDMA BEE

&

GRANDMA BEE
I AIN'T DONE YET

BY

HARMONY RAYNE

GRANDMA BEE

1. GRACIE ANN
2. UNSETTLING CIRCUMSTANCES
3. HOW MUCH MORE
4. CHANGES
5. BETTER DAYS
6. NOT AGAIN
7. ZEEK'S HOME
8. BITTERSWEET
9. IN THE MIDST OF IT ALL

GRANDMA BEE I AIN'T DONE YET

1. CHARLYE
2. MEMORIES
3. HARMONY
4. HARMONY'S FRIENDS
5. NOTHING HAPPENS BY CHANCE
6. THE UNREST
7. THE GREAT UNKNOWN
8. WISDOM OF GRANDMA BEE

GRACIE ANN

Journey with me as we get to know Gracie Ann. Born in small town Graysville, South Carolina, with a population of 3400. She is the oldest of five children, mother of six, grandmother to 13, and great grandmother to 10 with a heart of gold. Gracie Ann, also known as Grandma Bee, is a very intuitive, strong, courageous soul who experienced life in such a way many of us would have never survived.

Gracie Ann was born to an African American mother and a German Irish father in 1919 during the time period when racism, hatred, and violence was the norm against African Americans. The only knowledge of her father she knew was his race, which opened the door to pain, unanswered questions and the feeling of abandonment. Gracie Ann could not understand why her father didn't love her or her mother enough to take care of them the way a father should. After all Albert, Edwin, Jacqueline, and Emmalyn's fathers took care of them. He even left money for Mama June, Gracie Ann's mother, every once in a while. However at the tender age of 13 Gracie Ann's life would change drastically... It was a cold fall day the heavy downpour of rain that took place in their small town the day before caused flooding which made it impossible for the children to play outdoors. Gracie Ann sat sewing her paper dolls together. She gave each one of them names. Gracie Ann had such a vivid imagination and was serious about her master pieces, her dolls. So they each needed to have a name at least that's what Gracie Ann believed. She was what we today would consider an avid seamstress and dreamed of owning her own dress shop one day. She would often envision her boutiques lined up on Morris Drive, a much higher end part of South Carolina and where folk who had education and a good job lived. Her fun and thoughts was interrupted instantly by the slamming of the front door she thought to herself, dat betta not be one of dem chiren sneaking out. Especially after Ma got afte dem for asking to go outside. Gracie Ann opened her room door to see what all the commotion was. She couldn't help but notice that there were bags packed, her siblings were dressed and ready to leave. Ma what's going on, asked Gracie Ann? Why is everyone's bags packed but mine? With frustration in her voice and a cross look on her face, Mama June turned to her oldest child and said, Gal where's we's going ain't no room for a half white nigger gal. Besides you's old nough to take care yoself. It was in this moment Gracie Ann got a taste of reality that she wasn't prepared for. It was also the first time she felt her whole world being torn apart. Thinking in her head, what's I's done so wrong to be left behind? Gracie Ann stood there watching her family walk out the front door, into the black cab they went; all she could do was cry. With a broken heart she began to question herself. Asking, what's I's done so wrong dat my Ma would leave me behind? Am I's dat bad? Do anybody love me? Unfortunately, she was shocked but mustered up enough air as she screamed Ma, please don't leave me by myself! I's sleep in the trunk if you's want me to. I's be a good girl! I's do whatever you's say just don't leave me, PLEASE!

UNSETTLING CIRCUMSTANCES

It seemed as though what was taking place before her eyes was a terrible nightmare that she wished she'd wake from. All she had were her thoughts, her pain and loneliness. Standing there numb, lost and caught up in a web of emotions Gracie Ann didn't see when her older cousin, Henrietta, had come over. Henrietta was there to help her. As they, proceeded to gather her belongings the rain began to fall again. She went into deep thought once more. All she could think about was, Why me lawd, why? What's I's gonna do now? I's got only a third grade level of schooling. I's got no money and Mr. John gonna put me out cause I's can't pay him no rent.

As the days, weeks, months and years passed by Gracie Ann developed a thick skin for adversity. She managed to work through her feelings of abandonment and even managed to find work to make ends meet. By doing so she was able stay in the home in which she was born so many years ago. Gracie Ann's determination to make it without her mother and siblings drove her ambition to succeed. She had no other choice. Henrietta was there but she still missed her mother and siblings. She was a modern day multitasker. She worked daily in the house of the white man cooking, cleaning, and tending to their children doing whatever odds and end jobs she could get because she refused to degrade herself or be homeless.

Once more life would throw Gracie Ann a curve ball at the impressionable age of 17 her life would once again change. Like never before she had not been prepared for what was going to happen. Coming home from the corner market and a long day at work Gracie Ann was greeted by some familiar faces. A much unexpected site, it was her mother, brothers and sisters. She never thought she would ever see them again but low and behold there they were sitting on her porch. She dropped her grocery bags.

Wat's ya'll doin here, asked Gracie Ann? With sadness in their eyes her brothers and sisters turned to Mama June and said, tell her. Mama June swallowed hard and said, Gracie Ann I's needs to talk to you's in private. With anger that had been pinned up for so long she lost all judgment. She belted out, NO YOU'S DON'T! You's left dis half white nigger gal, meber? Filled with anger and rage Gracie Ann just wanted to know what they wanted. Why they returned back to Graysville? It's not like life had changed since they left 4 years ago. With desperation and gloominess in her voice Mama June tried to reason with her daughter. She replied, Gracie Ann please don't make me says it in front of all dese people. I's beg ya we must keep our family bness private. I's no secrets and nothin to hide, anything you's have to say you's can say it here in front of dese people. Dese people has becomes my family, says Gracie Ann. Don't you's forget I's still ya Ma and I's skin you's alive! Gracie Ann gave her mother a look that would shake hell loose.

In a very furious voice Gracie Ann replied, the only thang you's gonna skin is a coon.

"Very well then, replied Mama June. I's have a sickness that the doctor says dey can't fix and ain't no medicine working either. I's need you's to watch after ya sistas and brothas ya hea? I's gotta go back up to New Yak and go in the hospital and ain't no tellin when Imma be back for dese chiren. You's da oldest and you's da next person to tend to dem ya hea?"

Before Gracie Ann had a chance to respond her mother got back into the red cab and left for what would be the last time she would see her alive. She took care of her siblings as if they were her own and made sure that each one ate and got to school on time. She also wanted them to know that bible study and church service was something they would always do as a family. She promised her siblings that she would never leave them like their Ma left her. Gracie Ann also promised to see that each one would be educated no matter what she had to do.

HOW MUCH MORE

Two years had passed Emmalyn was in the 10 grade and seemed to be a great reader. One of the top readers in her class. So when the mail came Gracie Ann asked her to read it, because she wasn't as advanced as the rest of her siblings in reading. She was never able to go back and finish her schooling. There was a letter from their mother so Emmalyn was asked to read it. Gracie Ann was in fear, was curious and had a knot in her stomach as she anticipated what her sister would read in the letter. It read:

Gracie Ann,

Bys da time you's read dis I's be gone on to the Lawd up above. I's wanna say I's sorry for wat I's done to ya and how I's treated ya. I's scared to tell ya dat da reason you's not know yo Pa was cause I's raped wiles I's a yungin. Age about 10 I's think. I's knows if I's said anythang in dos days he'd kilted us both. I's angry most of my life cause when I's look at ya I's see his face. I's knows you's a reminder to me of him. I's pray you's find it in ya heart to forgive me one day and dat you's be a betta ma than I's was to ya'll. Da doctor says I's got somethin called cancer running through my entire body and it's only a matta of days dat I's be alive. I's can't tell you's who ya pa people cause dey run a large portion of Graysville and I's don't want dem to threaten you's or dem chiren. I's do ask dat ya keep dem safe and dat you's promise to raise dem close.

Ma.

Gracie Ann listened in disbelief with tears overflowing in her eyes. She thought to herself, how much mo can I's bare Lawd? It seems like life is getting harder and harder take me now, Lawd!

Edwin answers the knock at the door and yells to Gracie Ann someone's at the door for you. He says it's important. He has a teller gram. Hello madam, are you Gracie Ann Nesmith? Yes Sir, I's am.

I am sorry to sadly inform you of your mother, June Elisa Brantley, death at Racon's Hospital New York, New York at 7:00 am this 1st day of August 1926. We request your presence at the given place to identify her body and ask that you come as soon as possible. Your transportation and lodging is taken care of as well as burial.

It seemed as if her entire body went numb as she collapsed to the floor in disbelief. She couldn't help but wonder on the way to say her final goodbyes who was paying for all this. What kind of job did Ma have in New York, thought Gracie Ann?

Entering New York was something Gracie Ann never thought she would ever do especially in circumstances like this. As she arrived at the hospital she felt sadness, anger, disbelief all at once and it was weird she could not shed any tears for losing a parent.

In a bittersweet kind of way she was happy that her mother was gone and didn't have to live in pain or regret anymore. It was difficult for Gracie Ann to grieve over someone she barely knew. Nonetheless she stepped into mother/big sister mode instantly. She comforted her siblings and let them know she would never leave them and that she was all the family they needed.

CHANGES

As they buried and said their goodbyes to Mama June a cloud of sadness overwhelmed Gracie Ann. Yet she was determined to move on with her life. After all she was now 19 and dating someone who she believed was the love of her life, Ezekiel. He was a Private First Class in the Army who treated her like a princess every chance he got, when he wasn't away. Gracie Ann had been feeling sick for about a month now. Every over the counter medication she was taking wasn't working and she wondered what was going on with her In the back of her mind. She couldn't help but wonder if she had the cancer or if Ezekiel had brought her something she wasn't prepared for.

Mr. Draper, I's been coming to you's since I's was a little gurl. I's also brought my sisters and brothers to you's cause you's da only doctor I's got and trus wit us. Can you's tell me wat is wrongs wit me? Seems like I's done had dis flu for a month now? Is dis normal?

In laughter Mr. Draper looked at Gracie and said, I's noticed you's and Ezekiel have gotten pretty familiars wit ones another. He not from dis area is he? He from Darrensville not far from us but far nough. How'd you get mixed up wit dat nappy head boy? While laughing like a school girl Gracie Ann replied, I's met him one day walking from one of my jobs. He was in the grocery sto. He was a gentleman and helped me with my bags. He would leave money for me and the chiren and sometimes treat us to the movies but what dat got to dos wit my flu?

Gurl, you's pregnant! You's going be a Ma in bout six months. Dis flu not the flu. You's have what we know as pregnancy symptoms where you's throw-up, hot flashes, and you's don't have yo menstruation.

WHAT, replied Gracie Ann? The only thing dat was running through her mind was I am not like dose other loose gals, I's a lady and I's ain't given up my baby. I's sure ain't gonna force Zeek to marry me. Oh Jesus, we not married. I's can't do dis Lawd help me, Lawd! How I's pose to tell Zeek I's pregnant? In despair leaving the doctor office Gracie Ann thought to herself, God if it yo will for me to be wit Zeek I's will. I's not giving my baby up I's can't.

Days went by and then weeks went by before Zeek surfaced again. This time he would receive news that would not only change his life but everyone's life.

Butterfingers, which was his pet name for Gracie Ann, you's here called Zeek? Yea Zeek, I's right here. Why the long face? I's got some gud news and something to ask ya'll. Oh yea, wat gud news? Wat you's gotta ask us? Cause I's got somethin to tells ya and I's hope you's don't start no mess afterwards. Me first Zeek interjected, I's just got promoted to Sergeant. I's got a two dollar raise and I's saved enough money to move ya'll to Darrensville with me and my family. I's got a bunch of land and the chiren will have plenty of room to run on the farm and play. Butterfinger sit down cause what I's bout to ask ya is gonna change us forever. Breathing deeply and with a glimmer of hope and love in his eyes he asked Gracie Ann, will you's marry me? Without waiting for an answer Ezekiel placed the ring on Gracie Ann's finger. YES ZEEK YES, cheers of joy and spinning around from Jacqueline and Emmaliene. Oh Zeek, I's love ya and I's so proud of ya.

BETTER DAYS

For the first time in her life Gracie Ann was beginning to see a light at the end of the dark tunnel. Now what you's got to tell me Butter Finger? SIGH......... WELL ZEEK..... SIGH will you's says it already Gracie Ann! Alright alright I's pregnant and the baby due six months from naw! Waiting for Zeek to respond with possible violence, after all that's what she sees when the other ladies around town tell their lovers they pregnant. They get beat.

HOT DAMN, IMA BE A PA! Dat settles it we's going to the courthouse tomorrow. Gracie Ann was a bit surprised at his jolly response, yet relieved. Three days later on May 23, 1937 Gracie Ann Nesmith married Ezekiel Abraham Ellingsworth. On November 20, 1937 they welcomed their first child a girl, Ella Lorraine Ellingsworth into the world, 9lbs 3oz.

Ella would not only change both of her parents' lives' but she too would learn at an early age to overcome adversity and ridicule. She was a jolly baby and brought so much joy to her mother and father. Everyone spoiled her and her uncles and aunts fought over her constantly. Except for Jacqueline, that is. She was in charge of babysitting Ella when Gracie was at work. Jacqueline was at the awkward teenage phase and felt that her baby sitting duties was unfair and she was missing out on shooting pool, skipping stones with her friends and being able to go out without her brothers and sisters.

On a hot summer day Jacqueline noticed that Ella was turning blue She quickly ran next door to Mr. Draper's house. He had delivered Ella and was her doctor as well. He rushed over right away and sent

Edwin to find Gracie Ann because Zeek was away at war, the Vietnam War possibly. Praying like she never had prayed before Gracie Ann prayed for her baby she was a little over 9 months old and she just couldn't lose her baby now. As Mr. Draper came out of the room he told Gracie Ann that Ella would be fine. She had a bad case of pneumonia and he wanted to test her for another life threatening disease that can cause paralysis.

A telegram was sent to Ezekiel about what was going on with his family. He was immediately sent home to tend to them. Ella was not only a fighter but still the same jolly baby he had left just months ago. As the doctor ran the test both Zeek and Gracie Ann was hoping that their daughter wasn't paralyzed. Much to their surprise it was bittersweet. Ella got polio in her right leg and as a result would have to wear a brace on that leg for the rest of her life. Ella would be paralyzed in that leg only. She could still function as a normal child but with some special accommodations.

Gracie Ann saw this as an opportunity to thank God for sparing her child and that she would teach her daughter not to be consumed by her disability. She wanted her to fight as hard as she could to be just like anyone else. In fact she would teach her to be all that she could be no matter what.

NOT AGAIN

Time passed on and Ella finally reached grade school age. She would learn quite early on how cruel children could be and just how important it was for her to be the best person and student she could be. Ella was not your typical girl she was rough, loved any sports that involved physical contact, and also was considered to be what some call a "tomboy." Ella faced off with boys twice her age and size. She had even made a name for herself around school early on that she didn't take any mess from anybody. As Ella approached the fifth grade she had taken on the role as big sister because she now had another baby in the family that she would have to be responsible for. First it was Barry, her younger brother, who was just a year younger than her and now a sister, Pamela, who seemed to cry for everything under the sun. Ella knew that Pamela would be the dramatic one of the family after all she would cry and cry no matter what and when Ma would give her what she wanted it sufficed her. Gracie Ann still was working three jobs and Zeek seemed to be home lesser than normal because of the war and his role as Sergeant.

In fact, in Ella's mind it seemed every time daddy came home Ma would end up with another baby. Ella couldn't help but wonder how many more people would be living in there three bedroom cabin home? After all she was still sharing a room with Barry, who was a bit of a slob to say the least.

Winter went by and spring began to show its beautiful face. This was Gracie Ann's favorite time of the year. It is during this time that her and Zeek would take all the children fishing and would tend to their vegetable garden. However this spring would not be the same. It was in the spring of 1942 that Gracie Ann's world would be flipped upside down yet again. This time would scar her and her children for what would seem like a lifetime. The money stop coming from Zeek every month and Gracie Ann lost two of her jobs. Her last job did not pay enough for her to pay rent and buy food for the family plus the love of her life wasn't coming home anymore. Gracie Ann began to fear the worse, what if he is dead in that war and nobody came to tell her? What if her love was a prisoner of war? The kids kept asking questions where's Uncle Zeek? Where's pa? Gracie Ann didn't have any answers that would be sufficient for any of the children. She was left once more in a dark place that would consume her for what felt like eternity.

ZEEK'S HOME

Five years had passed since they heard anything from Zeek. Barry, Ella and Pamela were halfway through middle school. Emmalyn was off in New York pursuing the Army like her mother. Jacqueline was living in New Jersey with a friend she met working in a tobacco factory. Edwin and Albert were preparing to leave for the Navy in a week. Gracie Ann had so much on her plate that the stress of it all was overwhelming. All she could do was pray, cry and promise all the children that, "the Lord will make a way somehow." Edwin and Albert continued on with their plans and left for the Navy to embark on a life of their own.

Butter fingers, Butter fingers! Where ya is at woman, belted Zeek? I's need to see my sweet Butter finger. As Zeek searched the house in pursuit of his Gracie Ann he realized no one was home in fact the house was empty. It looks as if no one had lived there in some time. Zeek didn't know that Gracie Ann had packed up and moved back to what she knew as home. It was there she was tending to their children that he had left behind five years ago to the date.

Mr. Draper you's seen my family and my bride, asked Zeek? With a firm look on his face Mr. Draper said, don't you's come round hea asking where yo family is when you's done gone and abandon dem like deys ain't nothin. Gracie Ann been gone and I's ain't tellin you's wheres she gone, too. Mr. Draper slams the door! Somebody gonna tells me wheres my family is or else.

In a slurred drunken rage Zeek demanded somebody tells where his family and wife could be. Days and months went by with no success until one day a little boy who was in search of Barry came to the house. He told Zeek how he wished they hadn't moved back to Graysville. Just like that Zeek proceeded to head back to Graysville to reconnect with his family that he had been away from for so long.

KNOCK KNOCK… WHO IS IT, yelled Gracie Ann? It's me baby in a drunken voice. Baby, I's home and I's missed you! said Zeek. One would think Gracie Ann would jump for joy and run to embrace her love who she had been away from for so long, however Gracie caught wind to why Zeek had abandon her and their family. He had another family in Rockington, Connecticut. She took her frying pan and before Zeek could say anything WHOMP! GRACIE ANN ELLINSWORTH, screamed Zeek. Whys you hit me like dat? Dis da way you pose to greet yo husband?

Gracie Ann was so consumed with anger she continued to throw things at Zeek until her daughter Pamela grabbed her hand before she could do anything else to her husband and also because the way Gracie Ann was throwing things at her daddy it seemed like Jackie Robinson had nothing on her Ma.

Consumed with resentment, hurt and distrust Gracie Ann responded with a profound response and one that would become legendary in the future generations of Ellingsworth to come.

"I's a Christian woman who loves God, who obeys God's word to the best of my ability. I's not a whore, nobody's option and I's a woman of class if you's want to be a part of my life and dese chiren's lives you's will treat me in this manner. I's will accept nothing less than true love, honor and respect from you. If we are going to be together then it's time you act like it! If not there's the door.

BITTERSWEET

For the next three years Ezekiel and Gracie Ann went through a roller coaster ride of love, hurt, and pain. After the birth of Benjamin, Gracie Ann then decided she had enough of the back and forth. She tried hard to keep her family together especially since she never really had one of her own growing up but enough was enough. Gracie Ann demanded and deserved better than what she was getting from Zeek.

Ezekiel and Gracie divorced after 14 years of marriage. This not only hurt the children in such a way that Benjamin began acting out in school and Pamela was angry that her Ma made her daddy go away. Gracie Ann found herself once again back at a dark place and was beginning to think that God had forgotten about her. "God, I's pay my tithes, I's take the chiren to Sunday school and we's stay for church services. My brothers and sisters seem to be doing quite well for demselves yet I's left all alone with no ones to help me. What did I's do to deserve dis?"

As Gracie Ann sat on the park bench praying this prayer a young caramel brown man about 6ft 2in approached her and asked if he could sit next to her. She thought he was a breath of fresh air but he wasn't gonna know that at least not today thought Gracie Ann. Shrugging her shoulders she said sure and continued to pray and cry hoping that God would give her the answers she was seeking.

Excuse me ma'am, I's don't mean to interrupt you but I's couldn't help but notice a beautiful woman like you's sitting here in tears. Can I's buy you's a cup of coffee? I's guess so, replied Gracie Ann. I's don't have much time I's have to get home to my chiren. I's have four and deys expecting me. I's promise I's won't keep you long. I's just can't sit hea and watch a beautiful woman like you crying. By the ways my name is Fletcher Bronson, I's a Petty Officer in the United States Navy.

You's think that impress me? I don't care bout what yo job is and what you's do. I's need to get home to my chiren, sarcastically replied Gracie. Months went by before Gracie would run into Fletcher again. This time she was in a better mood and felt obligated to apologize for being so rude the last time they met and had coffee. As Gracie Ann got to know Fletcher she began to develop feelings she thought she would never feel again in life.

On March 15, 1959 Gracie and Fletcher were married in Morrisville, South Carolina and nine months later they would welcome a healthy baby boy Dixon Jerrone Bronne into the world. One year later they welcomed a beautiful baby girl, Charyle Luanne Bronson.

Ella, Pamela, Barry and Benjamin were excited about what would be the last baby in the family; in fact Benjamin would use his allowance money to buy his baby sister trinkets just because she was beautiful and lovely in his eyes.

Barry would hold her like she was as delicate as expensive China. Ella and Pamela saw this as an opportunity to boss someone around in the future and also Pamela would teach her how to be a girl because Ella sure wasn't, smiling.

The time passed, seasons passed, as well as the years and Ella and Barry were headed off to college. Pamela was soon to follow but would not finish in the same way Barry and Ella did. Pamela was more conventional and was overly obsessed with the Black Panther party in fact she use to say she was an "Angela Davis" kind of gal.

Benjamin the mischievous one of the group would forge his mother's name on military paperwork to go into the United States Marine Corp. He later would learn that this was not the best move to make especially at age 17.

IN THE MIDST OF IT ALL

On a hot summer night, 1969, Gracie Ann got a call that would rock and shake her world to the core. Barry was killed in an auto accident coming home from college. This was the worse news ever because two years prior she had buried Albert her younger brother and the only brother who seemed to be focused because that Edwin was a loose cannon who drowned while out to sea. Gracie learned that day that she had to maintain her strength and could not bring herself to tears.

While others comforted her after the funeral she felt empty and alone, yet she remained strong she had learned to mask her emotions and feelings at a young age and besides she had to keep it together for the sake of the kids.

Three years later during the summer of 1972 Benjamin came home from the Marine's and he came home married to Savannah Anne Crawford. Not only was Gracie Ann upset but Charyle asked Benjamin had he lost his mind. Benjamin and Savannah barely made it to two years before they were constantly fighting the only good thing about their marriage people would say are the two children Harmony and Aiden.

Aiden and Harmony would not only change Gracie Ann's life but she would treat them as if she had given birth to them herself.

As time and centuries passed on Gracie Ann would raise Aiden and Harmony as her own. She would live long enough to witness the union of Harmony to Kyle who in Gracie Ann's mind was the best thing that happened to her granddaughter. Harmony had a history of dating men who either were what Gracie Ann considered thugs, too fat or just down right not good for her granddaughter.

Gracie Ann also would get the opportunity to watch Harmony become a mother to two boys Kyle Jr and Kennedy. Gracie Ann, now Grandma Bee, reflects back on her journey in life and is proud of what her life has become. Grandma Bee remained strong with each challenge she faced and embraced each change that came her way with Grace just like her name. She loved each step from sister, to wife, to Ma, to Grandma Bee, and Great Grandma Bee... LAWD THANK YOU I CAN REST NOW.... Or can she?

CHARYLE

Mama are you home? Where are you, asked Charyle as she entered what she knew to be home? I's in da kitchen Charyle. Can't cha smell me cooking Sunday dinner fo tomorrow? Yall comin ova right? You knows how I's get bout my Sunday dinners and having my family wit me. Seem like I's just a ol emotional sap in my golden years since yo daddy died, Charyle. Dat man sure was a breath of fresh air to me. Sho we hads our differences and sometimes he would gets on my nerves so bad gal but dat daddy of yos was my pride and joy next to you churn.

With admiration in her eyes Charyle proceeded to the dining area where her baby grand still sat and where she also would create some of her most signature songs. Charyle aspired to be a songwriter and when she sang in the church choir it seemed like the heavens sang with her. Charyle reminisced on the first time Grandma Bee, or in this case mama, had saved up enough money to pay for her piano lessons. Bronson bought her the baby grand and would sit in his rocking chair on Saturday afternoons listening to his baby girl tickle those ivories; is what he would say. Charyle felt as though when Bronson was around listening to her play that she was on top of the world. She loved her dad so much she after all she was his baby girl. When he was around she felt like she was queen of the world and the only thing that mattered to her was her daddy. Charyle would play on her baby grand for hours on end. There were times she would be so into playing she would play past dinner time.

As Charyle sat at her now out of tuned piano she thought about all the times she played on her prize possession. She recalls the heart breaks, anger and frustration she would take out on her baby grand she realizing how therapeutic playing the piano was for her until this very moment.

Charyle thought about her first love her daddy. She played one of her favorite songs "A Song Just for You" by Donny Hathaway. Charyle was a huge fan of Donny amongst others like Stevie Wonder, Prince, Michael Jackson and Sade. They got her through some real hard times.

Despite her piano being out of tune Charyle played her song as if she was in concert by herself. As the tears began to fall down her face she played louder and more intensely. She really was missing her daddy and Sunday dinners just weren't the same for her anymore. Mama, why do we still have Sunday dinners if daddy is not at the head of the table anymore? It just didn't make sense to her to carry on as if her father was around. With discontent in her voice Charyle shared, the only people left locally are my family, Dixon's family and Mama Teat. Mama Teat was Gracie Anne's foster mother who was now suffering from Alzheimer's disease. Gracie Anne didn't have the heart to place her in a nursing facility especially since she knew Mama Teat didn't have any real family of her own.

Harmony had moved more than 1000 miles away and was now having Sunday dinners with her own family. Aiden kept getting himself into trouble and was now living in Sparrowsville to get himself together with his girlfriend Regina. Grandma Bee once again was hopeful that Aiden would finally grow up and get his life together. After all she wasn't getting any younger and he was getting to old to be living life as if he was invincible and as if the world owed him something. Pamela's children Melinda, Ramona, and Duncan only visit during the holidays. Jermaine who is Ella's only son was living somewhere up north. No one knew exactly what he was up to unless he called Grandma Bee. He only called for help when he needed to get out of a jam he had gotten himself into.

Gal listen hea and listen gud; alls my life I's wanted to has my own family. Cooking, laughing and making family memories dat I's could take wit me to da grave and some I's could pass on to yous and yos churn. Yous thank I's don't kno yos daddy gone? Yous thank I's don't thank bout him ery day? Tis been 5 years. Mama Teat aint gettin no betta; I's don't knos nothin else but to loves people, to help people and to jus give my heart. Da good book says, God is love, and all my life I have tried my best to teach yall about God and the power of his love. Besides yo daddy would want me to tinu da tradition of dis hea family.

I's often sits hea and think about Harmony and Aiden and a part of me is so proud and da other be so sad sometime. Harmony went through a lot wit dat Benjamin of mine and Savannah Lord knows dat chile would cry herself to sleep. No matta how much I's would tell her to be strong seem like she was on a mission to save her parents. Lord knows I's thought she was gonna have a nervous breakdown chasing behind Benji, Savannah, and dat Aiden. Wit tears in her eyes Grandma Bee wiped her face and continued to mix her batter for the upside down cake she was making for tomorrow's dinner. Charyle kissed her mother on the forehead and said see you tomorrow mama, I love you. She realized in that moment just how caring, unselfish and giving her mama was and thought to herself God has truly blessed me with a jewel for a mama.

One cool brisk Sunday morning Grandma Bee got up put on her, what they call down south her, Sunday's Best. At age seventy something, a lady never tells her real age, she got her breakfast ready, put her Sunday dinner on low heat and headed off to worship service. After all she was the Sunday school teacher for Orange Road Missionary Baptist Church. She had been a part of this ministry since she and Fletcher married so many years ago. They were one of the first members when Pastor Harris opened the doors almost 20 years ago. He's sweet I know. Storm clouds may rise, strong winds may blow, was the song that not only ushered the presence of God in Sunday school but one of Grandma Bee's favorite hymns. She would sing this on Saturday's as well when she was preparing Sunday's dinner. Nothing like cooking to the sounds and tunes of the

Lord she would say. As Grandma Bee sang to her heart's content in Sunday school she thought to herself I's am so proud of Charyle. She is tickling dos ivories and da heavens are singing and shouting wit us dis beautiful Sunday mawnin.

Charyle was the church's choir director, organist, and hospitality coordinator. Charyle's eye for fashion and flare for music is just what Orange Road needed. Like Grandma Bee Charyle knew how to open the heavens in praise and worship. Dat sure was a fine sermon pastor, I's like dat very much. For the wages of sin is death but the gift of God is eternal life, yes lord yes! We gotta let dat Lord have His way in our lives da way yous shook da devil today, YESSA! Fletcher would be so proud and jumpin up and down yous knos dat Deacon of yos was known for leapin in da spirit when yous be preachin. Yes ma'am he did, Sis Bronson yes ma'am he did. He was one of the best deacons I had and could pray. Charyle stood in the distance as her mama and Pastor Harris reminisced on how special her daddy was. He was the epitome of what a real man was to her. Mama what time do you want us over for dinner? I have to run to the store to pick up some drinks but we'll be there. Okay baby be dere by 4.

MEMORIES

One of the greatest memories Harmony had was how Grandma Bee would prepare Sunday's dinner on Saturday. How she would be the one cutting up the fresh okra, shucking corn or cleaning the shrimp while Grandma Bee shared some of her life stories with her that she would carry with her into her own family. Now being a 1000 miles away life would not be the same for her. She would learn fast that having a family of her own meant you create your own family memories and traditions. It was nothing like being back down south walking down the street to visit Mrs. Timpson, Mrs. Timmins, or Mrs. Colson. Mrs. Colson was famous for her red velvet cakes and shrimp and grits. Harmony was best friends with her granddaughter, April, who later would follow in her grandmother's footsteps and open up her catering shop with her husband Darren.

Mr. Chuckle Berry is another beloved neighbor, his real name is George Nile Chuckle Berry. He was named after his great grandfather who in turn was the first successful black business owner in Morrisville. Mr. Chuckle Berry graduated with a Master's Degree in Science. Many parents would look at him strange when he would do science projects with the neighborhood kids. He was so daring and full of adventure nothing seemed to scare this man.

Mr. Chuckle Berry was the guy all the neighborhood children adored. He would bring candy, cakes, and play pranks on people that sometimes caused him to lose friends. Mr. Berry would say, I'm just having a little fun. Loosen up a little why don't ya. He believed that people took life to seriously. Mr. Berry felt one never lived if their always following rules according to man's law. This is the one of many life lessons Harmony learned from Mr. Berry. Another was not to take life so seriously all the time. Harmony also learned to live to your own beat, fulfill your dreams, be comfortable with who you are and to never settle for anything less than you truly deserve. Despite his awkward ways he truly was a wise man in her eyes. She kind of wished he was a part of her extended family and not just a neighbor.

HARMONY

The telephone rung. Grandma Bee looking like who da devil is calling while we's eatin dinner? Hi grandma it's me, Harmony. I miss you guys so much. What's for dinner? Oh hey Harmony da family jus gathering in to eat. I's put on a pot of beef stew and made some fresh string beans. You's know I's need my nutrients. I's baked a pan of cornbread, made my pineapple upside down cake, and some homemade lemonade to wash the stew down wit.

How's ya liking da weather where yous at darlin? How's Kyle and da churn? Grandma Bee was so happy to hear Harmony's voice especially since she moved miles and miles away from home. She remembered how hard Harmony and her best friends, Monica, Josie, and Arbury, cried when Kyle packed the last of Harmony's things in dat U-Haul truck. You's had thought dey never see each other again da way dey carried on.

The weather here is weird one minute its freezing cold, then it's hot, and the next minute it's raining cats and dogs. Kyle's work schedule is crazy, the kids are adjusting pretty well by making new friends, and so I can't complain at all. I just miss those Sunday dinners we all use to have. Well grandma, I will let you get back to dinner because I know how you enjoy chatting and eating with the family. I love you guys and I'll call in a couple of days. As Harmony hung up the phone all she could think about is how special those family dinners really were to her. She never realized just how important they were until leaving home and living on her own with her own family. She was happy to have a family of her own and a husband who was supportive yet she missed those moments of eating Sunday dinner with her grandma. She missed the smell of pine in the fall from her grandmother's backyard and most of all she missed the convenience of being able to go to any seafood restaurant and indulge in her blue crabs and shrimp.

Harmony was a proud military wife and mother so she tried very hard not to complain a lot or make a fuss when Kyle Sr. would come home. He was gone from his family a lot and it often put a strain on the marriage. After all he is a high ranking NCO in the military and has to deal with situations that many civilians wouldn't have the patience for. So as Kyle Sr. was preparing to deploy yet again he would be missing Kyle Jr. and Kennedy's birthday and their 6 year anniversary.

Harmony wasn't new to him being deployed or doing his FTX, field training exercise, yet she felt alone. Her frustration levels were at an all-time high. Kyle Jr., now five, felt more independent than ever and felt cuddle time was for babies. Kennedy, soon to be four, was curious and finding things to color on which included the walls, countertops as well as the outside carport. To top it all off out of all the articles she had written and submitted to 40 newspapers only three responded with news that she didn't want to hear. How was she supposed to keep the family and house together and still keep her sanity? Nonetheless she was thankful for her two little ones and excited to see what her future would be like with her beloved Kyle.

Harmony kept remembering what Aubrey had told her the night before she left. Remember you are a wife now and you have to live your life with your husband your way. Build your own family, create your own memories and remember you don't have to do everything our parents did in their marriage. We are different and unique.

HARMONY'S FRIENDS

As Harmony sat and thought of her friends; Monica, Josie and Aubrey all she could do was smile. Of course she was the encourager, motivator, and the big sis of her circle. Monica who lived in Tennessee now was preparing to launch her latest book "Black Love." She and Harmony have been friends for more than 15 years they shared the love for writing and poetry together. Harmony loved how Monica had the ability to bring words to life and how she could go from character to character with a breeze. Josie was the most responsible one of the crew. She and Harmony had been friends just as long as Monica and Harmony. Josie would always share her financial tips with the crew. She has her own accounting business in Michigan and is doing so well with her husband, Randal. He is an engineer. Their expecting twins this summer and Harmony cannot wait to be there to meet her twin nieces. Aubrey and her husband Obey were living in the suburbs of Richmond, VA. She has just passed the bar and will be joining her husband in the grand opening of their new law firm in the spring.

It seemed as though all of Harmony's friends were doing so well but she was struggling to be recognized as a freelance author and writer despite her BA degree in Psychology. She wants to be a medical writer, a short story author/playwright, and eventually open up her coaching practice upon graduating with her master's in education in a year.

As Harmony gathered Kennedy and Kyle Jr to go to the local park for a playdate with friends she thought to herself something has got to give. I am a good person, I'm kind, and do my best to live a life pleasing to Christ and one my grandma can be proud of. Why does it seem like my dreams are just that, dreams? Am I just a dream chaser? Will I achieve all that I desire to achieve or will I depend on my husband for the rest of my life? This is not what a help meet looks like somethings gotta give thought Harmony.

Harmony feels her cellphone ringing but can't locate it right off. Finally, hello MONICA? Hey girl how have you been? Girl I almost hung up figured you were sleeping or something. I'm sorry I had my phone on vibrate and forgot to change it back. You know I can't remember our time difference. Brighton and I have some awesome news to share with you. Really, what's the exciting news? Let me guess you guys are moving my way? WELL ... Are you sure you're ready for this Harmony, Monica replied trying to keep the suspense going for her friend. Out with it already missy the suspense is going to make me crazy. Okay... okay with excitement Monica shared that she was engaged and would be getting married later in the year. She asked Harmony to be her matron of honor and not to say anything because she hadn't shared the news with her family yet. Harmony felt honored and was so excited that Kyle Jr and Kennedy looked at her as if she had lost her mind because of her loud scream of joy. I would be honored to be in your wedding and congratulations to you and Brighton. As Harmony chatted away with her sister from another mother she thought to herself this conversation is like a breath of fresh air and just what she needed. The news that Monica shared with Harmony gave her the boost she needed to shake off the pity party she was beginning to have.

NOTHING HAPPENS BY CHANCE

She took her children to their playdate where she would soon learn the concept, being in the right place at the right time. Excuse me ma'am, is your name Harmony? Depends on whose asking. Why? I am Sterling with On Top of the World Publishing Company. I read one of your articles you submitted to a friend of mine's magazine The Beat. I found your article intriguing and have been trying to contact you for weeks now. Don't worry I am not a stalker. Yes, my name is Harmony and it's good to hear that you're no psycho because I'm a pretty tough cookie myself. I know how to hulk smash if I have too. How can I help you Sterling? I would like to offer you a writing job with my publishing company. Do you do short stories and can you be flexible in your writing style? Feeling as though she was dreaming Harmony thought to herself, is this really happening right now at this very moment? Coming out of her daze she replied yes of course I am flexible. I am the kind of writer who likes to keep her audience in suspense when I have too as well as motivate change. I believe there is power in our words. Great! I know you're busy so is it okay if I get your information so that we can set up a formal interview and meeting so that we may bring you aboard? I promise I'm not just selling you a pipe dream and there is no catch.

Let me call my husband, Kyle, real quick said Harmony. She quickly called Kyle and put him up to speed with the events that just transpired. I tell you what after you fully discuss it with your husband and you're still interested here's my business card call me on Monday. Harmony didn't know what to think or feel. She took his card and couldn't stop smiling. Is it possible that the very thing she had desired ever since the age of 12 was about to become a reality? Was this the big break she was looking for or needed to get her masterpieces out to the world? Harmony couldn't wait to get home to share this exciting news in full detail with Kyle and then with Grandma Bee. She just felt on top of the world and knew that this would be a moment in her life she would never forget. Kyle was excited for Harmony and as they prayed together before bed Kyle gave Harmony a look that would melt her soul. Harmony thought to herself that's the look that got us these two children.

Harmony was not prepared for how her world would be turned upside down when she called home to share her exciting news with Grandma Bee. Hey grandma! How are you guys? How's your week been? With excitement Harmony was waiting for Grandma Bee to share her week with her and then share her exciting news about her writing job. WELL..... Not so good suga; I's in sum pain. My head hurtin and we's trying to get all da information from yo mama Savannah bout Aiden's accident. I's jus don't know how's much mo I's can take in my old age Lord knows Aiden, Benjamin, and Jerone has had lives like cats. WAIT WHAT, REPLIED HARMONY? WHAT DO YOU MEAN INFORMATION ON AN ACCIDENT FROM Savannah?" What's going on grandma? Calm down suga I's didn't want to call you until we's had all da news. It seem dat Aiden not wit dat gurl no mo and went to where ya mama is months ago. Member da last time we spoke I's told ya it was crange I's hadn't heard from him? Yes grandma, I remember but I'm scared what's going on? Savannah called us two days ago saying Aiden was in a motorcycle accident and his condition wasn't good. I's jus waiting fo da news to what hospital he in so dat we can get to him. Lord knows I's love dat boy as my own son. It seems he jus keeps living life on the edge dat gonna kill him one day ya hear? GRANDMA I'M COMING HOME! Now now no need fo ya to up and come home cuz of dis honey I's keep ya posted and if we need ya to come home we will go from dere. Now what's ya news ya seem so excited. Harmony had completely forgotten about her good news after hearing about her brother. She was nervous, scared, and angry all in one. However she refused to show it or let her grandma know. Well I got a writing job and I could start as early as next week. I'm excited about it and Kyle is too. This could be the break I have been looking for grandma you know. Dat's wonderful darling! I's so proud of how you turned out and I's admire yo

determination. You's one determined gal. Well I's going to lay down now I's talk to ya soon suga.

Yes ma'am, I love you!

Harmony didn't want to wake the kids so she did her best to gather herself she tried to

reach Kyle but was unsuccessful. He was due to leave for deployment, for 12 months, in two days.

The last thing he needed to know was his wife was a basket case upon leaving.

> Dear God,
>
> It's me Harmony I know I haven't been faithful in attending bible study and Friday night
> service at church. I am coming to you with a broken heart and scattered mind asking
> you for strength for my family as Kyle deploys and as I embark on a new job. My
> brother Aiden is not doing so good and I'm sure you're up there, like I know Harmony
> I'm omnipresent, but can you please allow him the chance to live and get it right with
> you before you take him?
>
> Amen.

With tears in her eyes Harmony stared out her kitchen window trying to process the news she just

heard. All she could think about is how she needed to keep it together not only for herself but her

own family. As much as she loved her brother she realized that she could not wallow in fear

especially since all the information was unclear at this point.

The telephone began to ring, hesitantly Harmony answered. Hey grandma that was fast.

Swallowing hard Harmony waited for the news. Aiden is wanted in Brunsfield for larceny at a local

clothing sto. Savanah came and got him in hopes he'd do betta in a different place. He's stayed wit

her only four days befoe he went chasing fo drugs. As Grandma Bee tried to keep herself together

she shared wat had happened. Harmony was consumed with a deep sadness and just wanted to

curl up in a ball and die. He was wit sum fellas who is local drug dealers. Seem dat he was riding

wit dem when dey was chased and dat's how da terrible accident took place. Da doctors say he's could be paralyzed. Not sure if it will be forever or a lil while but either way he not doing too well. Grandma Bee was known for being a woman of strength and the one most people came to for prayer and guidance but this time it was Grandma Bee that needed strength from Harmony. "Harmony can you sing a song with your granny please? Sure grandma whatever you need?

Harmony reflected on how her and Grandma Bee use to sing on Saturday mornings when she would have to prepare for her social gathering meetings. Grandma Bee was a part of a Christian Social Club that helped youth and poor families in the community. Each week they would rotate whose house they meet at, would bring a dish, and discuss their community service for the month. The level of joy Harmony felt singing His Eyes Is on the Sparrow, The Lord Will Make a Way Somehow and Amazing Grace with her grandma felt like old times to her. Time passed and Aiden was paralyzed.

THE UNREST

Harmony would learn during this year that her marriage wasn't what it was cracked up to be. Kyle had been gone now for 8 months and was 4 months away from returning home hopefully with new orders to go somewhere else. Kyle Jr. and Kennedy were a year older, taller, and were becoming more active in sports. Harmony was in a good place in her writing job and was even promoted to manager. She was contemplating writing a novel but that was still in the air. She was enjoying doing blogs for local restaurants and revamping short stories from other authors.

The news Kyle shared with her would not only change their marriage but their family's life. How could they bounce back from this? Would this tear their family apart? Hey baby, I can't wait until you come home and we can make up for all the lost time. Harmony, I have something to tell you and I need you to listen to me without interrupting or asking questions. Okay, what is it babe? Well, I got offered a position that will put more money in the house and when I retire will have us set for life! Kyle was known for being a guy who thinks outside the box and one who got things down without hesitation or being asked. Really? This sounds exciting what is it? SPECIAL FORCES. They are giving us higher enlisted NCO's $80,000 sign on bonuses to be a part of Special Forces for at least three years. I already took the job and I go to school for training about a week after I am home from this deployment. Harmony promised not to say anything and to hear Kyle out. However the frustration she was feeling was almost unbearable. You there love? Yes. So what do you think? Are you excited? We moving on up! How's work going for you? Harmony took a deep breath. She shared how she was happy that Kyle was given an opportunity to progress in his career but she was not pleased with him not talking it over with her first. After all this is what married couples do right? The fact that you have been gone a year and will only be with us roughly a week when you return makes me very upset and angry. At this rate the boys will never know who daddy is. I see your being emotional and in your feelings right now. I will call you in a few days, I love you. Harmony not only was angry with Kyle she wanted to bop him upside his head for making a life decision like this without talking it over with her first. Did he not realize how this would affect them and their family? Did he stop to think about the fact his boys are growing up before his eyes and he is missing all those special milestone moments? She understands that the military is a demanding career and she would have to share him with Uncle Sam. Yet never in a million years did she imagine her husband would do Special Forces especially since she shared with him years ago her dislike for this part of the military. Nonetheless Harmony prayed that God would take her anger away and to show her how to be a supportive wife for her husband.

Harmony heard a loud thump. What are you boys doing down there Kyle Jr.? Nothing replied Kyle Jr.. Harmony knew that nothing with her two active boys meant something and in most cases something needed to be fixed or was broke. Harmony went to assess what the commotion was about and didn't have the strength or energy to make a fuss about the boys breaking her favorite wine glass and tinker bell figurine. Kennedy was surprised that Harmony didn't make a fuss or even flinch. Is mom losing her mind Kyle, asked Kennedy? She's not even flinching? Pretty weird if you ask me. I'm not sure Kennedy but don't bother her just go with the flow maybe she's too excited to fuss because daddy will be home in 24 hours who knows. Either way she didn't whoop us for that. I am thankful! Kyle and Kennedy cleaned up the mess they made and couldn't help but wonder what had gotten into their mom. Could it be that their mom just was not stressing anymore?

THE GREAT UNKNOWN

Time passed and Kyle Sr. came home and went on his training for his new job. Little did Harmony or Kyle know that it would be a long while before they would see one another again? Days, months, and years went by and Kyle Sr. was gone. Harmony did her best to tell the boys why daddy wasn't calling or coming home anymore. Eventually she had ran out of excuses and depression began to set in for her.

It had been five years since Harmony had heard from her beloved. She had spent thousands of dollars in trying to find her husband but to no avail. Kyle Jr. and Kennedy were teenagers now and had long stopped asking for daddy. They just assumed he wasn't coming back. Both had developed a dislike for the military and blamed the military for taking their daddy away. Kyle Jr. came running in the house with mail that seemed top secret and important. He gave it to his mom and waited with anticipation of what was inside that thick orange folder. Your father is alive Kyle Jr., screamed Harmony! He has been a prisoner of war in Saudi Arabia. One of his battle buddies was able to escape. He sent me all the letters your daddy had written to us for about three years. It says here in one of the letters, by the time you read this I may be dead. They keep torturing us and my ability to sneak and write to you is becoming slim. Straight up, I'm scared and all I want is to hold you in my arms, look my boys in the eyes, and kiss my momma and sisters.

Kyle Jr., Kennedy, and Harmony looked at all the letters with hope and sadness at the same time. At least now they knew that Kyle Sr. couldn't call or write them because he was a POW, prisoner of war. Kennedy saw his dad as a hero and Kyle Jr. was ready to go find the people who had took his father from him. The doorbell sounded and Kennedy answered the door. It was a man of average height who was at the door asking for their mother. Kennedy wondered who this man was in this blue uniform. Where is my dad thought the boys? What do you know? Why are you here? These were questions they had but out of respect for their mother waited for her to signal them to come into the dining area of the home. Hello Harmony, my name is MSGT Higgins, I was your husband's direct supervisor. I am coming to share with you that he is alive and will be released in three days from Saudi Arabia. Though I cannot tell you in detail what his mission was it was strictly government confidential. I can tell you I am proud to have worked with your husband and honored to say he stood strong in the midst of being a POW.

Listening contently to what this man was sharing about her husband so many emotions went through Harmony's mind. The times she felt all alone, the times she had to deal with life struggles without her husband, and last but certainly not least how her friends and family would pressure her to just move on. She couldn't because in her heart she felt her husband was somewhere out there waiting to come back to his family. Her faith in God, her Grandma Bee sharing scriptures and prayers with her is what kept her and got her through life's storms. She often would think about when she and Kyle started dating and how they planned their lives forever. She held on to forever because it was what she meant when she said I do to Kyle almost 15 years ago.

Harmony I need you to listen to me carefully. Kyle will not be the same and it is quite possible he will not know any of you because of the torture he has had to endure and has experienced in the last five years. So, what you're telling me is you knew where my husband was all this time and didn't bother to tell me? You, asshole, do you realize the trauma, the pain, and unanswered questions my family has had in the past five years? Do you understand I have spent thousands of dollars trying to find my love only to find nothing? How dare you waltz into my home as if it's just business and share all this information with me and expect me to be calm? All I want to know is when and what time do we need to meet my husband? You sir, have done enough damage to my husband and family now get the hell out my house and face.

WISDOM OF GRANDMA BEE

Kyle Jr. knew the only time his mom would go off like this was when it was something serious. He quietly went in his room to call Grandma Bee because it was evident that the only person to calm his mother would be Grandma Bee. Harmony thought to herself now how am I supposed to feel? She was so overwhelmed with emotion and fear.

Now Harmony Rayne ya listen to me, I's not pleased wit how's ya handled yo'self wit dat man today. I's know ya upset but carrying on in dey way ya did is not Christian like. If I's were dere I's would had bopped ya one. Yes ma'am, I was just so angry and I couldn't take his smug look anymore grams. Chile ya has got to learn not to let people and things dictate ya responses. In life ya gonna deal wit some hard thangs but ya gotta let da Lord have his way. Let Him fight ya battle ya hear me suga? Yes ma'am. Now go on and apologize to dem churn and keep me posted on Kyle ya hear? Yes ma'am, bye grams.

What Harmony didn't know was how much of an impact her Grandma Bee had on each member of her own family. Kyle Jr. loved visiting her in the summer time for a week and helping in her garden or around the house. It was in those moments he gained life lessons that he could carry in his heart forever. Like the time he asked Grandma Bee about dating girls and how she shared with him that girls come and go but for him to always be a gentle man and to pick his lady friends wisely. Kennedy was over the moon for his grampty. Her cooking was food for his soul. He loved how she would bake his favorite desserts and mail them to him in Arizona at football camp each summer. He couldn't imagine life without his grampty even if she was 92. For Kyle Sr. it was the advice she gave him that time he wasn't sure he and Harmony would still be a couple that he held onto the most. He held on to it during those long gruesome years as a POW.

Kyle darling let me tell you something: the joy of the Lord is your strength, always keep what the good book says in your heart.

Psalms 91 "He who dwells in the most high he will protect. "The Lord is the strength of your life whom shall you fear?

Love covers all. It was this wisdom and advice that Kyle held on to as he hoped that he would one day come home to his family. Despite the daily branding he faced to his back and legs he held on to Grandma Bee's words of wisdom and he often would imagine her singing and cooking just to get through the day.

Harmony how's Kyle adjusting to being back? Is he crazy or no? Well grandma he has nightmares and sweats a lot. The doctors are testing him for PTSD. PTS what chile? PTSD grandma its post-traumatic stress syndrome. It's something soldiers and people can get when they have been faced with trauma. Oh okay. Well your Aunt Charyle got a concert coming up and I's was wondering if you all was gonna come to support her? Yes, sure I think we all could use a trip home. It might jog his memory of who everyone is. He still struggles with the boys sometimes. Okay well I's gotta go get my meat out the oven. I's makin meatloaf for Sunday. Pastor coming ova wit Deacon Bright to discuss renovating da church.

As time passed on Kyle Sr slowly began to recognize who his family was. He began to recognize when he was experiencing fear in public. He continued to hold on to what Grandma Bee said to him, I'm still holding on to God unchanging hand for you son. Kyle Sr. was severely traumatized and retired shy of twenty years but with high honors and a purple heart. It wasn't until they visited home to see about Grandma Bee after her major surgery that everything started to come together for Kyle. He remembered asking for Harmony's hand in marriage at this house, he remembered some of his best homemade meals and holidays were here, and most importantly he remembered how Grandma Bee took him in with open arms shortly after marrying Harmony as if he was already family.

Dear God,

It's me Kyle I know I haven't talked to you in some time now and in fact I have missed a lot of time with you. I know that your real and I'm asking you to give my bride strength as she watches her grandma recover from heart surgery. Lord you truly blessed me with an angel. She could have left me but she stayed and embraced me with love like no other, even after all this time. Grandma Bee is the rock of this family and I just don't know what will become of this family if she's not around anymore. Benjamin is a mess and even though he's my father-in-law he still needs his mama. Aiden will be lost without Grandma Bee and the boys would not know what to do without their grampty.

Amen.

Harmony couldn't help but reflect on how amazing her Grandma Bee truly is and how much wisdom she continues to share with everyone she meets. She was most thankful that Grandma Bee surgery was a success and now they were awaiting her to come home from rehab. Harmony holds on to what her granny said to her prior to surgery the Lord ain't through with me yet and I ain't done yet!

www.ingramcontent.com/pod-product-compliance
Lightning Source LLC
Chambersburg PA
CBHW020953030426

42339CB00004B/89